R.F.D. IOWA

A Collection Of Poems

Myrna Sandvik

Ice Cube Press
North Liberty, Iowa

RFD Iowa: A collection of poems

ISBN 9781888160260 (1-888160-26-8)

Library of Congress Control Number: 2006928636

First Edition

Ice Cube Press
205 N Front Street
North Liberty, Iowa 52317-9302
p 319/626-2055 f 413/451-0223
www.icecubepress.com

Manufactured in the United States of America

∞ The paper used in this publication meets the minimum requirements of the American National Standard for Information Sciences—Permanence of Paper for Printed Library Materials, ANSI Z39.48-1992

"Sweet Fruits" appeared in the *North American Review*; "Cat Eyes", "Seasons" & "Red-Winged Blackbird Migration I" appeared in *Lyrical Iowa*, in slightly different form.

To my mom and dad,

Georgia and Walter Pierce,

who walked this path with me.

TABLE OF CONTENTS

R.F.D. Iowa: A Collection of Poems was written to celebrate and share the rich Iowa culture as lived on a traditional family farm, a way of life that is rapidly disappearing from the Midwestern landscape. The poems are a series of glimpses or snapshots of a life that stemmed from these rural beginnings.

Foreword

It all comes back: the Indian arrowheads, the old pony express trails; bumpy pastures and one-legged stools; Uncle Orr, the water witcher who never fails to find water, and Grandma's green glass canning jars. Sandvik's *R.F.D. Iowa* gifts us poems postmarked from our past, but speaking to our lives today. She creates an autobiography in forty-six poems: "snapshots of a life that stemmed from these rural beginnings." The poems appear here in a kind of photo album, with tiny photographs of rural life drawing us into four sections. "Rural Heritage" (with its enticing enjambments) leads to the closely observed "Rural Childhood." Sandvik then examines "Country Meets Town" only to return us "Back to Nature" where she clearly feels most at home.

Readers from "R.F.D. Anywhere" will resonate to coon hunters and to the love for a tractor, to sledding down hill on a worn scoop shovel, to scattered hay on old snow. However, the "sandhill cranes grazing the wetlands," and references to Jefferson and Lanesboro reveal the poems' Iowa ties. Like Czech composer Anton Dvořák, who immortalized Iowa's scarlet tanagers in his 1893 "American Quartet," Sandvik, too, is drawn to birds—and birdsong. For her, maple trees are "convention hotels" for redwing blackbirds, but only momentarily, for she then captures redwing migrations, their "churning wings and flashing tail feathers." Many Sandvik lines offer the compressed beauty of haikus: "Silent snowfall drifts/through brown grass and tired stalks/burying autumn." And in the starker "Iowa Nile" that captures our floods, she shows us "leaves hanging from bent stems: broken promises/surrounded by rubbish caught in fences."

In "Country Meets Town" the poet measures rural America's current challenges: "the giant corporate farm/that already cages us in on three sides." In "Downsizing," she chronicles in diary form the closing of the Aurora plant, and then the Churdan plant—all to the bitter public relations refrain "all will be well." Nevertheless, in "Remembering the Family Farm," the section's opening poem, we see how farm habits live on in town, while "Ode to Fast Food" digs at bloated (and bloating) McDonalds. That Sandvik neither complains nor directly attacks, but simply observes, only makes us feel more powerfully the terms of our loss.

—Barbara Lounsberry

Barbara Lounsberry is a Professor of English at the University of Northern Iowa. She was named the University's Distinguished Scholar in 1994. She is particularly interested in the subjects of Midwestern life and literature. Born and raised in Iowa, Professor Lounsberry believes Iowa culture, like its soil, is incredibly rich.

RURAL HERITAGE

History

The magnet of the past pulls me as I hike
through the bumpy pasture on the farm where I grew up.
I stop at the deep, wide groove that slants up the hill.

My dad told me this rut marked the old pony express trail
and I imagined the nights of riding through snow
with hooves sliding on the steep hillside and icy

north wind gusting down the riders' necks as they rode south
and east to Lanesboro and Jefferson. Dad was sure
the trail was also the stagecoach road for several years

because it was the easiest place for struggling horses to pull
the loaded coaches up to the ridge from the river valley.
I roam on to the spongy spot on the hillside

where small springs form miniature waterfalls for a season,
then shift over a few feet to start a new rivulet
for the following summer. In this ideal camp space

my brother and I found an Indian arrowhead once.
It is easy to imagine the long ago confrontations
along the trail fifty feet away. Eventually I cross

the patch of fuzzy-leaved beans, pooling knee-deep in the field
that was virgin prairie. I remember when I stayed home
from school to help Dad plow and disk it.

I bumped over large furrows so deep the plow could not
turn them completely over. For days I climbed the tractor
over one giant solid wave until it collapsed, and rode

on through the trough to begin climbing up the next one.
I was always ready to jump over the uphill tire if the angle
became so steep the tractor would start to tip.

Hands in pockets, I cut through the now-ordinary field
to the far edge where the river bank becomes a wildlife zone.
Fluttery birds are hunting for weed seeds and insects.

The tall burrs and underbrush are cut by a track that fishermen
follow to the river. I remember when 'coon hunters ran
with their baying hounds almost every night

if the moonlight was bright enough to see the river's edge.
One day soon, the romance of living amidst familiar
history and nature will end. My dad will be forced

to honor our neighbor's option and these acres will become
an unheeded part of the giant corporate farm
that already cages us in on three sides.

The Iowa Nile

Only a family who farms the rich bottom ground
recognizes the threat of too much rain about

late June or mid-July. It seems a godsend to folks
whose land is high above the flood. Their jokes

about "too much of a good thing" or "corn too tall
to pick this year" somehow aren't funny at all

when the rain for miles will flow downstream
to destroy knee-high corn and ten-inch beans.

My father's reaction was always the same,
first a slight frown when hearing of more rain,

then drumming fingers as the river starts to rise,
resetting his cap, saying this was the year for rice.

While pacing a track in the living room floor, he goes
from window to window to see how clouds are set

and if there is any let-up, especially to the north
where creeks come roiling down, a mixture of both

water and mud, a deadly brew for young crops
to be submerged a week, until the river drops

back into its banks and drains away, leaving
only fetid puddles and dead stubble, decaying

leaves hanging from bent stems: broken promises
surrounded by rubbish caught in the fences.

Soon damp dirt begins to crack in the hot sun.
The mud bakes hard, too late to transplant

this time. But only my die-hard-farmer father would,
in face of ruin, looking for a way to do some good,

settle on mending the sagging fences for spring
when he could try for that bumper crop again

with luck next year. He cleaned his way through
twenty yards of debris, when knee-deep in muddy slough,

disgusted with hard luck, sick from stench and muck,
blinded by anger, he took his hammer and struck

through the water. To his complete surprise
he hit a twenty-six-inch fish between the eyes.

It's true, the crop for the year was merely a wish,
But, that night for supper, Mom cooked the fish.

Filling Jars

Mother's pressure cooker sang
As we picked the pea pods
And green beans from the garden.
Our dew-drenched clothing
Chilled us all morning
Until the sun finally burned.

From first harvest to winter
The empty jars were all fed
With the best of every crop. Their maws kept
Us harvesters hustling. All day we
Climbed apple trees, peach, and pear in the orchard;
Picked cucumbers and cabbage from the ground.

The broccoli and squash came late,
Carrots were dug, and by autumn
We'd picked ripe watermelon and cantaloupe
And stored them in the garage until frost.
We gleaned last bits of tardy crops
And knew we'd won

Our harvest, and when the snow
Drifted our lanes and buildings,
We knew we'd eat well this season.
Until late spring there'd be many choices,
And even through mud of thawing,
Our jars would provide until planting.

Spring Fever

As soon as the Christmas tree
is put away on New Year's Day,
and the last thank-you note written—
sometimes before the very last one—
my mother gets out dozens of titillating
seed catalogues and starts dreaming
of the summer garden. She doesn't stop
with her perfect plan though.

She buys tomato and cabbage seeds and
starts the baby plants that will grow up
in her garden. She makes small beds
from cardboard milk cartons cut in half.
In an inch of soil she plants the tiny seeds,
puts the boxes in cake pans, and covers

everything with plastic wrap—a greenhouse
nursery where tiny sprouts soon become
too crowded. She places the larger ones
in old egg cartons, with a tablespoon
of potting soil in each little pocket.
If she uses up her egg cartons
and has to buy peat pots, it is a minor

failure, as she likes pots to cost nothing.
She sets the cartons and pots and paper cups
to drip into jelly-roll trays and cake pans
until she has the whole counter full
of two-leaved plants basking
in her attention—watering, fertilizing,

weeding—waiting for the warm
spring day, when she can move her adopted
children to the garden to play.

RURAL CHILDHOOD

First Kite

My first kite
was made from forest
green tissue paper
with slender balsa wood
struts slotted for the string
we glued around the edge
of the diamond shape.

When it wouldn't fly
but nosedived into the dirt,
Dad said it needed a tail.
Mom let me tear strips
from my outgrown pink
sundress that already had
a hole in it.

The next time I sent that kite
into the blue spring sky,
it shivered slightly in the breeze
with that hot pink tail
shimmying like
a hula dancer.

Whiz-zzingging

On the way to drive
the cows to the milking
barn, I'd find small flat

stones to juggle as I walked,
and throw them at the road
signs later. Or sometimes

I'd try to hit the glinting silver
telephone wire betwen
dark wood posts on fragile

glass insulators—a tempting
target. The stone whizzed
out and missed, and missed

again. At last, I heard an echoing
ZZINGG that vibrated and
hummed the line for at least

half a minute. After practicing,
I heard the WHIZZ-ZZINGG almost
every time I threw carefully

chosen game stones. Maybe the
neighbors noticed static in their
phones, but they probably didn't

know they might be living by
the best WHIZZ-ZZINGG player
in the whole darn world.

Winter Games

I watch the disciplined Olympic
skiers in their streamlined
suits weave graceful slaloms
and remember the day Dad
showed me the thrill of flying
downhill on a worn scoop-
shovel with a hand-me-down
coat flapping around my arms
and worn Levi's freezing stiff
as snowmelt hardened in the
arctic wind.

Sweet Fruits

after Gwyn McVay

In the core of the apple there are five seeds.
A scale weighs out the bananas,

green, golden, spotting a bit
as they ripen. We can't remember

their dry sweet taste when thirst drives us
to go seeking a cold nectar

of tomatoes, ripe squirting seeds and flesh,
the cool juice in the mouth like a libation.

Apples roll from the counter.
A guilty child hurries to his mother's side.

Hurrah, the Cat is Dead!
(A Tale of Catastrophe)

Of course, we sang "Hurrah, the Cat is Dead"
When Nellie's one-eyed, broken-tailed tomcat died.
"Too bad he only had nine lives," Nell said.

He once was squeezed in springs that bounced the bed
Where the neighbor's dog drove him to quickly hide.
And so, we sang "Hurrah, the cat is dead."

But when a howling, spitting fur ball sped
Across our feet, we knew our song had lied.
"I'm sure he only has nine lives," Nell said.

Nell dragged his tail as she lugged him by his head;
Dog jaws and horse hooves battered his rumpled hide,
Again, we sang "Hurrah, the Cat is Dead."

But back he bounced to the careless lives he led,
And pained young Nell with every death defied,
Because, "He only has nine lives," she said.

One fatal day he chose a tire top for his bed
And restful nap became half-circle ride,
In truth, we sang, "Hurrah, the Cat is Dead!"
"It's sad he only had nine lives," Nell said.

The New Mailbox

The mailbox is a lovely thing
All mounted on its fancy post.
The snowplow hits 'til early spring.

Advantages our hearts must sing
Though ordinary and plain to most,
Our mailbox is a lovely thing.

We hope that winter will not bring
Deep drifts around the box like ghosts,
The snowplow hits 'til early spring.

December's mail holds cards and gifts.
We sing our happy Christmas toast,
The mailbox is a lovely thing.

January's mail and box take wing—
Twenty feet and more they have to coast.
The snowplow hits 'til early spring.

In March the plow uproots and flings
The post, with mail all wet and lost.
Our mailbox was a lovely thing;
The snowplow hits it every spring.

Uncle John's Ninetieth Birthday Party

Uncle John was naughty, natty, and ninety—
a big stallion of a man with white rippling
beard and a mane that just touched his collar.
For his ninetieth birthday party he made sure
he had a date, and flirted outrageously with all
the ladies. He wanted everyone to understand
that he could still make the dating scene.

John's son Tom was the racehorse of the family,
who left the farm and became a big-shot broker
in Sioux City. When he blew home with his
trophy wife, Tami, in his show-off sports car,
we hadn't seen him for several years, so we
chucked the farmer jokes and pulled out the
awkward sophistication we use for city folk.

John's daughter Susan always pulled her share
of any load. She rented the hall, baked the cake
and bought her daddy a new shirt. All day,
she set tables, decorated the room, made coffee,
washed dishes, kept the party alive, and took
significant pictures. Later, she wondered why
she couldn't remember a visit with any of us.

Triplet Saga

rub-a-dub-dub rub-a-dub-dub
three carefree toddlers in a tub
sitting grandly two inches deep
in a tepid swirly sudsy sea

Mommy's and Granny's tough
hands vigorously rub and scrub
holding off pending mutiny
of able-bodied small sailors three

Kyri licks pearly soap and feels
crescents of dents from small teeth
Carson drowns a squealing duck
and soon hugs six squirting frogs

The red frog sprays Colton's face
beginning a short splashing chase
when the scrambling gets too rough
Mommy's frown says that's enough

Granny drains the high-tide down
Carson yells out he's not quite done
lunging to reopen the faucet's flow
he hits the cold shower knob below

swaddling towels mute crashing
crescendos of waves splashing
untuned screams and dripping hair
ending triplet sailors' tubside tour

Recipes from Four-year-old Chefs

Carson's Leaf Sandwich

Find a really nice leaf
Make some gooey mud
Use a short stick to cover the leaf with it
Find another good leaf for a lid
and put it out for the rabbits to find

Colton's Grass Cake

Find a big pail
Put in grass and sand
Pour in lots of water and mud
Stir with a big long stick
Try to find some crushed leaves to put in
Add dirt and make it squishy
Let the mixture set for 2 or 3 days
Decorate it with short sticks like candles
When it smells done, Mommy or Daddy
will tell you to dump it out for the birds

Kyri's Mud Pie

Take a big handful of mud that isn't too squishy
Make it into a ball
Roll it in sand until it is covered
Pound on it to flatten it
Set it on a board in the sun
It will get hard so you can throw it at things
and crumble it up for the squirrel

Downstream of Summer

Evening of forgotten last Tuesday morning
earned by sleeping soundly on through noon. Fuzzy
brain until I met you to lunch and shop; we
spent more; knew better.

I feel addle-minded and unrewarded
when I slowly push the cart into blue-lighted lanes,
peer at bargain prices; another shopper's
win and I'm bitter.

Restaurant, a luncheon to rest our minds;
salads with crackers and no-fat dressings:
autumn specter haunts us with dread of school's grind:
plans made, we move on.

I buy pens and folders and you, lined notebooks.
We soon grab erasers and pencil boxes,
fitted out with crayons and rulers—relive
childhood daydreams now.

Plan to spend most every lunch together,
though our shared classes are many. We can
plan clothes, gossip, finish our homework. We say
"Sisters forever."

Water Witcher

Uncle Orr was a water witcher. His magic
hands knew where water flowed. He told
all the neighbors where to dig their wells.
Pacing his grid across a field, holding
his witching stick before him, he'd say,
"Stake this line. Dig anywhere on it.
You'll hit water. Best spot is right here."
He would mark the dirt with his heel
and walk away. There was always water.
He never missed.

After family campfire stories, I cut the fork
from a small sapling. At wedding procession
pace, I stepped onto the bridge, and joked,
"If I were Uncle Orr, I could tell there is water
here." Over the water, the wand quickened
in my hands. Above the stream, it twisted
and pointed straight down. After crossing
it was lifeless. The boys tried, but the stick
was dead. Again and again I witched.
I loved the magic.

Green Apples

They left the tree with a snap
Of stem before the bitter first taste,
When sour juice curled my tongue
And pinched my puckered lips so tight
My whole face was contorted
For the sake of July's hard ritual.

August and again I tasted the old orchard's
Half-dead trees, to see if they filled up my hands
And whether they held promise. Biting from one
And leaving the rest to ripen some more,
I felt the autumn stirrings and knew
That time and sunshine again

Would give their rich reward. The yellow cat
Chased bugs and grasshoppers. The small birds
Had flocked elsewhere—knew they weren't ripe.
Three weeks later, in the same neighbor's orchard,
I carried the ladder on one shoulder,
Set it below Eden, climbed toward the sky.

The owner's wrinkled face stared at me,
Chilliness oozing from set mouth and eyes
As I looked down from where I gripped the tree
And gasped and knew. When the screening leaves stopped
Rustling, while our eyes met, I held out hands
Filled with forbidden fruit I had to return.

Debris

after Gwyn McVay

Downpouring, a stream swelled up
by the rain to flooding stage,

the banks of the riverbed gone down
beneath the swirling brown whirlpools

that sweep along their wake of leaves,
and dead but green trees, wilting brown,

a bent kettle, a stump, mud-washed canning
jars of the green glass Grandma preferred,

milk bottles, rusted cream cans, a knot
of baling twine holding a nest, empty

but round still, a dead pig rolling sideways,
its curled tail uppermost: other people's disasters,

the sorrow which sympathy generates.
Water an enemy; water a friend—its present

overabundance, a flow of negative zen.

COUNTRY MEETS TOWN

Remembering the Family Farm

The love for a tractor grows up with farmers' boys
Who see Dads astride their romantic, loud machines.
Sons stake out miniature fields that suit their need
To practice farm work with shiny scale-model toys

That move real dirt and make a growling sound.
The tricycle pulls the small red cart of grain
Pedaled to tend pigs and hens, time and again.
Sharing farm chores gives Dad and Son a bond.

But the farm must be sold, and city Son now feels
His love for long straight rows, from the seat
Of his small tractor which bags grass, spreads peat,
Pulls the clattering mulcher, and scatters seed.

He knows a brown lawn won't lose the cash crop
But pride in his almost-farm won't let him stop.

Commuter Marriage

I stand housecoated
in the doorway feeling
your hasty kiss, damp
on my cheek, and notice
dawn's first rays burning
my sleepy eyes. Dimly
I see your fluttering fingers
through the foggy windshield
as we disconnect for the week
to come. I drift back to empty
coffee cups and the faint smell
of your aftershave, unready
to cast off the weekend's
afterglow.

Ode to Fast Food

The endless line
before
one gets to order
all the gourmet
delights.
Two sandwiches
with everything
dripping
to our laps.
Quarter pounders
with sesame seed
fill our mouths.
Whoppers, char-broiled beef,
salted fries,
vanilla ice-cream cones,
McNuggets,
all tasty,
but bring an urge
for a lady-like belch.
We'll eat on
'til it's gone.

Raw onion
cuts the bland
ketchup and mustard
flavor
has faded,
once blended, they
disappear,

cancelling
each distinct flavor.
A tart green slice
of dill pickle
becomes the final taste.
Curly fries
in foldable box,
herbed, but limp
as cold spaghetti.

Chocolate shake
cools my mouth,
then moves on,
fills my stomach,
chilling mass
that starts a headache.
A large coffee
thick with bitterness
burns
first my tongue
and all through my chest,
but at last
becomes cool.
When we leave,
our bloated minds
resolve this is the last time
intense hunger
leads us
so astray.

Telemarketer

the telemarketer calls
i'm startled awake   make a grab
the phone falls on the floor
is mr sundrack there
no mr sandvik is at work
can i help you
never mind   i'll call back
when it's more convenient

next day   same time   another call
both my hands are full
i drop my daughter's picture
is mr sundrack there
mr sandvik works weekdays
can i help you
never mind   i'll call back
when it's more convenient

next day   twenty minutes sooner
i've just started my shower
i slip on the soap   i nearly fall
is mr sundrack there
no, he passed away last night
in great pain   can i help you
never mind   i'll call back
when it's more convenient

Cat Eyes

You look at me with cat eyes that
question and turn away as if
ashamed to have doubts, but

I do not know the answer you
seek, nor do I understand
your question,
unless

it is how we can live with unfinished
dreams we can not fit into
our frantic lives, or

why our private space is filled with
attempts to connect that
seldom match.

The Accident

after Edward Byrne

I remember the white color
in the bustling hospital
and the way you looked

squinting through the cloudy
oxygen tent, squeezed nostrils
wearing the hoses like
earrings. You still wore

the bunny sleeper. The small
fingers of your chubby hands were
not grasping at my hand.

Your mitten string had tangled
around your hands like handcuffs.
The broken branch dropped
onto the lawn—a stalwart support

suddenly failed. I was surprised
that you did not cry out
(In my mind you are always

screaming from the fall
of the swing.) The people
on the sidewalk and roadway
quickly ran, to help you.

Some stood nearby. One asked
whether you were breathing.
A few green leaves fell like hail

from the restless storm cloud. A boy
with unruly dark hair falling
over intense brown eyes looked up
into the tall tree to see

what had happened, but he could
not really tell. A young man with an apple
and sandwich unwrapped in his hand

ran screaming, "Call nine-one-one!
Nine-one-one!" I didn't
even know if you felt my
holding you. The only smell

was grass. The ambulance
pulled up on the sidewalk
and you were taken inside.

I rode in the front seat,
giving history for their records,
told them, "today you said you'd love to
ride your swing up into the sky."

Last Free Lunch

Adam and Eve
Became too smart.
No reprieve,
No paid leave,
Monday they start.

Downsizing

Friday, November 8
The state of the business report disclosed loss due to many
things.
The oil price hike increased costs of materials. Customers had
added
expense as well. The economy is bad for industry now. We'll
tighten
our belts and work harder. After we re-price everything,
all will be well.

Friday, November 15
The Aurora plant will be closed to become a central
distribution
point. Two people will stay to handle shipping and receiving.
Everyone else—except twelve people—bids for jobs in the
tech
center and the Churdan plant. With this small change,
all will be well.

Friday, November 22
Today our manager chairs a meeting to discuss new economy
measures—work groups reorganized, cubicles rearranged,
jobs traded—until his 9:30 conference call. We talk trivia
until noon when we hear he has resigned. With him gone,
all will be well.

Friday, November 29
One-third of the people in the tech center were laid off.
We kept all our good workers; dumped the dead wood.
They'll get two-months' severance pay and counseling.

That should get them through Christmas—
all will be well.

Friday, December 6
Twenty-two people were laid off at Churdan.
Unanswered phones ring on empty desks.
No Christmas party this year. No lunch group.
Who's in charge? Who tells us all is well?

Friday, December 13
—is tomorrow.

The Gerbil

A gerbil would be a nice pet
the family agreed for once.
Small, inexpensive to feed,
clean the cage once a week.
Not much else.

Or so we thought. First of all,
the children could not agree.
So we came home with two.
Still not too bad, we thought.
Until too late.

Two gerbils turned out to be a pair,
which is very different from two
gerbils. In a few short weeks we
owned twenty-eight little balls of fur.
They kept coming.

Soon all the friends of the family
had at least one or two little critters,
whatever traffic would bear, and we
procured more cages to have girls'
and boys' dorms.

Which worked somewhat, except that
none of us were expert at gender
sorting, and even worse, it was hard
to remember which cage Sue or Sam
belonged in.

In spite of occasional lost battles,
we gradually were winning the war
by furnishing lovely pets for each
classroom in the school and every
interested child.

When we were down to a single gerbil,
one child bought his own pet cat,
which was always locked carefully
away from gerbil land, until the final
disastrous day.

Prayer For Daughters

after Lucille Clifton

make them be macho
make them be lost in the dark
but need to be on time
let there be no gas station

let their advice be confused
and lead them in the wrong direction
so they must turn around

later there will be flashing signs
and roads in the dark
leading nowhere. let them
ask for help if they
aren't afraid of muggers.
let them try to find
someone they can trust

let them think they can read their map
and that to ask for help is dangerous.
let them get hopelessly lost
with only themselves to advise.

The Woman Who Loves Lawn Ornaments

after Lee Ann Roripaugh

If you come to see my lawn
 to look at all the art,
you might have to peer about, as I'm

often hidden among life-size statues.
 They look real at first glance
and almost seem to move around

in hide-and-seek games. I do not care
 that much for flowers
and shrubbery. They always die

or have to be pruned every week
 to keep them the same,
as they grow in perverse patterns,

wilting from their trellises, running
 roots to other places,
and exploding in a blaze of color-

clashing good health. (Even Buddha
 would lose his patience.)
And so I prefer not to

trouble with growing bushes, pulling
 daily weeds from every plot,
knowing they will not stay beautiful

unless I keep working—some mulch,
  some water, fertilizer.
I love my pink flamingos,

the long lines of small ducklings
  that march right after Mom
to the reeds by the pond.

When my glowing lighted fountain
  must be emptied in the fall
and the gray, ugly tank is exposed

to winter—I must fill it with
  Santa's reindeer flying
over the steep sides, and pulling

the sleigh above the snow
  and ice—but I
most love the little donkey

who pulls his cart in one place,
  and never rests.
I have a flock of woolly lambs

and some geese which turn in wind,
  their tails aflutter from the breeze
they face, my silhouettes of people,

who appear to work among the animals,
  the old windmill with its whirling blade,
just behind the weather vanes.

I polish them all in their turn,
  they stay where I put them and move,
when I decide where. So reliable,

my whirling daisy.

My ceramic hen.

My cement deer.

Second Honeymoon

We wave farewell from the packed car and shyly
Grin, feeling strangely naked, without children
Between us. Just Leonard and Myrna again—
No more need for busy Mom and Dad. We try

To believe family was not the glue that bound us
To each other. We leave the silent house after
Feeling older made us choose a traveling adventure
Alone, together. Awkwardly we walk in step, as

The quaking path brings us to endless, untuned
Roar that drowns our voices, fills our ears
And brains with awe, while our eyes just stare
At Niagara, priestess to couples. Still communing,

Following the bank downstream, our senses
Slowly grow alert to the park's normal detail.
We see a tired-looking man, cane on the railing,
Smiling at young honeymooners, when

Three times his hand swipes his eyes
Before undammed tears stream down his face.
"Are you all right? Can we help?" "No, please,
My wife and I come every year. Now she dies.

I come today to keep the memories. She's gone."
His shoulders fall and he shrinks smaller.
Thoughtful, we three watch the tumbling water
Fall. He says, "Today, I know my life is done.

Go now. I want to think of Anna. To be alone.
You are young. You have your whole life to do."
We leave him, not really sure that we should go.
Together again, we float through the crowd, as one.

Warning:

Low-Maintenance Road
Enter at Your Own Risk

The mag-wheeled Cadillac bounces
from rut to rut, wide tires scrabbling
for a footing in long grass, giving out
a crushed green smell. Sparse gravel
melts to bare dirt, where once was
a wide smooth road ending in home.

The road becomes a corn field just beyond
the sagging gate. A rusting *No Trespassing*
sign clings to a broken-down fence, crushed
under slanting iron posts. Two girls teeter
on fashion heels and follow the deer trail
over the fence looking for their childhood

farmstead, stopping where streaked gray
walls and roof tops, have sunk below tall
weeds and encroaching corn. Memory
can repaint the molding walls sparkling
white, but cannot help the returning sisters
find their old ball diamond and tire swing.

Striking Buddy

The set crew spent weeks crafting
a Fifties world, complete with small-time
radio stations and the Surf Ballroom,

dressing scenes with old-time music
stands and microphones. We thought
on the twist with poodle skirts swirling

above bobby socks, and saddle shoes
fast-stepping through carefree gyrations
invented a generation ago when moving

hips fast with neat feet on the beat
was cool, man, cool in worship of magic
drumbeats and gutsy guitar solos.

The cast relived it nightly with packed
houses as Buddy's name ignited memories
and his thumping music shook up our souls.

The nostalgic run was too soon ended—
encores and standing ovations rang
the curtain down, with the impact

of a crashing plane. We scurried to move
props back to their dusty corners while flats
were converted into lumber for the next

imaginary world. We ravenously scooted
across the block to the strike party where
we would eat, and remember, and forget.

The Trip Back

We enter the familiar, well-watered
Platte lowlands on our way back from
Kearney, knowing we will soon see
sandhill cranes—hundreds of them—
splashing in ponds, grazing the wetlands
for grass seed, gleaning muddy, long-
harvested corn fields for stray grain.

After several watchful, uneventful miles
Leonard, puzzled, says, "I know this is
the right weekend. They've always been
exactly here in the middle two weeks
of March. They follow the Platte all
the way up their spring migration trail;
and finally rest in these marshy bayous."

We watch the small ponds and bent
brown grass with drooping seeds,
and see nothing else. I glance up
into the clear sky and spot them—
ragged flocks, moving like clouds—
not the wide Vs that ducks and
geese keep—but loosely organized

squares, like billowing patchwork
quilts with a few blocks missing
in each one, holding their air space
until they start endless clumsy landings.
Group after group parachutes roughly

down—each crane a feathered balloon
that bounces on impact and snatches

at the nearest ripe clusters of seeds
before regaining its feet. At dusk,
we cross the Platte to drive scenic miles,
sharing our evening with the cranes that
cover the landscape like a lumpy blanket
over a squirming, not-yet-sleepy child.
We talk of the happy "Nebraska Days"

of our early marriage, remembering the awe
of two small boys on our annual family
pilgrimages down the Platte Valley to see
the "big birds" and picnic in the refuge.
Surprised how soon the time has passed,
we stop in Council Bluffs to rest and dream
of the river valley filled with roosting cranes.

BACK TO NATURE

Revisiting the Old Barn

Grandfather's spirit seems to hide in the dust,
his lantern and one-legged stool in their place
on iron hooks, long, red, and scaled with rust.

The cows and cats have gone, surrendered their space
to raccoons and mice who welcome the shelter
and give the barn some purpose in its old age—

like my volunteer retirement job I'd prefer
to think has use—but not like bygone days
when cats risked all for one squirt of milk before

the machine took over the chore that Grandpa always
did by hand. This year the robins have a nest
on top of a stanchion in the milking space,

and swallows flit through the windows to rest
on the concave ridgepole and in the mud daubs
they've plastered to wood-pegged rafter and joist.

The wind hums in the drafty haymow, and a dove
coos the dance tune for two dust devils that cast
gold chaff on the scene of Grandpa's final jobs.

Red-Winged Blackbird Migration I

By twos and sevens,
blackbirds claim their branches
and rasp grating welcomes
to new arrivals,
until three large maples,
become convention hotels,
fill with the raucous
assembly.

When arrival is complete,
rowdy discussions are
suspended while the flock
flutters down and scatters
like a fall of black leaves
to peck and scratch,
gleaning nearby fields.

Dinner foraged,
dark shadows flit back
to evening accommodations,
where rustlings and twitterings,
speak of the sunset,
and early checkout
with the dawning light.

Red-Winged Blackbird Migration II

One strand spirals to the sky,
threading tight curls into sea-blue,
soon joined by another swirling strand
winding upward, weaving a moving
knot of glowing colors glinting
sharply where the sunlight glances
from churning wings and flashing
tail feathers. String after string rises
to weave itself into a billowing
tapestry that blankets the sky
from horizon to apex as it slowly
drifts above ripened fields sectioned
by tree-choked streams.

Dusk unravels the tiring flock,
loosing a strand downward to feast
on ripe grain. Another plummets
like loose lint into welcome branches
above freshets of clear water.
Evening stars and rising moon
shine clearly through opening
rents in the disintegrating
fabric. The sky darkens
as the last ragged remnant
glides earthward to spend
a cold watchful night in
haphazard roosts.

New threads emerge at first
warmth of early sunlight,

to reweave their kaleidoscopic
designs in endless natural
patterns above square fields
and crowded streets.

Seasons

Golden moonlight glints
across wind-sculpted snowbanks
silhouetting deer

Damp earth smell, new grass
tempt lilac blossoms to spill
deep purple perfume

Ripe red strawberries
hidden in jagged dark leaves
attract blue jay's bill

Pink and orange leaves
whisper Halloween secrets
to shuffling shoes

Silent snowfall drifts
through brown grass and tired stalks
burying autumn

Winter Scene

moonlight spills onto
snow-lit porch railing and stairs
stippling the house

cedar tree shadow
forms the darkly hidden tent
for two young rabbits

snow-molded footprints
wind through rows of naked trees
to a hollow trunk

windstill wintry air
holds a black, night-gliding owl
over his shadow

ice-coated grass stubs
puncture loose drifted snow piles—
shining golden spikes

Fall Dance

Knit one, purl two
Arabesque and turn
Quick pas de deux
Behind the stitch

Yarn over and purl
En point, turn, pause
Leap, split, and whirl
Whip on down front

Rib knit the wrist
Final crescendo
Needle ballet finished
Warm mittens adieu.

Cricket

As I gather the fall crop
of squash, potatoes and
the last few green beans,
I enjoy the seasonal chirp
of the garden cricket
until

I hear him happily singing
from the vegetable bin
just inside the family room
door. I dread stalking him
and cringe from the final
crunch.

Haiku

Fireflies light the field,
Short-lived insects wink at night,
Competing with stars

Robin flutters off,
Brown hiking boot just grazes
Three nested blue eggs

Yellow and brown leaves
Whirl in the wind, uncovering
A ripe black walnut

Robins dart under
Tractor and scratch black furrows,
To snap up pink worms

Tired boots leave warm car
Skid on ice under new snow
Wave in frosty air

Scattered hay on old snow
Meager meal for twenty cows
And one starving deer

Fresh grass, daffodils,
Tulips and new leaves hide two
million lady bugs

Deer

They gracefully leap eight feet high
those magnificent, athletic deer.
How can I resist their shy amber eyes?

The dog looks clumsy as they dance by;
his frantic chase ends far behind where
they elegantly leap eight feet high.

Across the fence, silhouettes against the sky,
they prance to the woods and disappear.
But I remember those bright Bambi eyes,

that seem so innocent, shy, and naive
masking the impulsive hungry deer.
Uninvited, they chew an eight-foot-wide

trail of destruction. I see in dismay
my plants and trees ruined forever.
Easily now I resist their charming eyes.

From my once-beautiful garden, I cry,
"I'm building a tall fence yet this year.
Just gracefully leaping eight feet high
won't gain this prize for your greedy eyes."

Morning Coffee

Dewey back steps are prime bleacher
seats for the early morning matinee.
Our birds greet us with eye contact
and turn on professional performances.

The sparrows romp by in rowdy
waves pecking and twittering down
the lawn. They shove and tumble,
squabble over tasty morsels, and carry
away dried grass and twigs.

The sky is filled with swallows
that fly in with fancy swoops and rolls
to buzz our heads, hungrily catching
insects on the fly, and enjoying their
own graceful aerial acrobatics.

A male robin is calling territorial
challenges to other contenders
who answer from nearby perches.
Coy females look on, shyly
reserving their favors.

The bright redheaded woodpecker
whose echoing din from staccato
pecking on the metal machine shed
roof is the show stopper. He proudly
outclasses his rivals who beat their beaks
on hollow trees. Performance over,
he flaps his way to the low limb

beside us to bow and preen before
remembering some other business,
he flits off across the lawn.

Fire Start

Outside, I light my fires
without the show-off poof
of lighter fluid or the flashing
tongue of gasoline that scorches
my sleeve and vaporizes leaves
on near-by saplings,

but with one match, patience,
and small wads of paper or dried
brown grass. The nearly invisible
orange flame crawls slowly
along the surface, gradually
biting deeper

until the color changes to cherry.
Hot blue flames support spreading
yellow patches and snapping sounds
when kindling flares. Amid sharp pops
from green branches, I work up
to larger chunks

for the satisfying roar of wild
flames devouring giant logs,
while the hot, hungry wind bears
the sweet smell of charred
wood and thunderous clouds
of roiling smoke.

Along the Gravel Road

after Marilyn Hacker

I leave my Tuesday lunch break having relearned
at least a habit, not yet a ritual.
big combines, slower tractors run by
harvesters sweating in long-sleeve work shirts.

Streams, soft as sea foam, vibrate aboard, like
rain swollen, crested, half-wild waterways—
always reflecting the spouting changes
as they fill the wagons and borrowed grain trucks.

Three German Shepherds nap in the wagon beds,
shovels and canvas covers dropped next to them,
down the slope of field in the rutted
dirt track, safe as suburban children,

while, underneath the shade tree, a grouping:
red cattle, horses like Italian marble,
two ponies, dappled brown and gleaming auburn,
chew grass quietly, snort and move on.

I bring letters to read in my favorite
chair, well-shaded by trees near the balcony
over the backyard. Sometimes swallows
glide up and settle over the doorway.

Shit! someone's pulling right into the drive
in my free time . . . I'm not able to stay relaxed.
I'm sure the pickup is a strange one
so I get up. It pulls around back

to the doorstep—an aggressive salesman,
pert, pat, and pushy, shoes gleaming black, soft light
suit, fancy case, and fake tight smile,
stomping his feet like a proprietor.

He clomps up, sits down, thrusting his fidgety
brown, sun-tanned hand in front of me, a weapon
that I have to grasp until he has finished
telling me all about the humid weather.

Who welcomes, leads him on in, closer to the
door, even asks him what he is selling now?
I don't, although he's tried two times, his
serpentine smile curled to draw me in.

He stands and leans expansively on the balcony
railing, attempting to capture my interest.
I glare and watch him, wishing him gone,
stolidly resisting his gambits.

Eternally he offers the same worn-out
remarks, never touching my needs or desires,
until he, recognizing his foolish
posture, shuffles out, defeated at last.

So I forget him, turn back into my life.
As do the animals in the sunny silence.
We sit, not knowing and never caring
at all what gadget he might have sold us.

Cousins

Sparrows, brown fluffy balls of feathers,
sit gossiping and preening in the sun,
resting from the summer of three broods,
each fed tons of fresh weed seeds,
and spilled crops. In spitting snow,
their short, flippy wings beat their way
to shelter in the drafty barn. Staccato
chirps die as they fidget to keep warm.
Roosting in the high rafters, they wait,
for summer and perfectly round homes
of grass trimmed with string and down.

Swallows, sleek, thin world travelers,
vacation away the unpleasant winter,
arrive in May with graceful swoops,
diving on streamlined wings built for aerial
acrobatics in impromptu performances
for their mates lightly perched on swaying
highwires. They slap quick daubs of mud
on last year's fixer-uppers, briefly tend
new chicks who must learn worldly ways
by August to leave in the next migration.

Early Snowstorm

after Edward Byrne

Today, the early snow darkens the old photographs
        on the table inside the window, and as skiers
trek across the country, we relax in the calm
        and peace of our rockers beside red-glowing stoves
that warm our quilted toes. The gusting wind,

harsh this winter, swirls the slow drifting snow
        our balcony holds along the railing,
during the calm moments drops misty sparkles
        silvering dull spots that sag along the wall.
In our warmth, the whine of the wind echoes

around us—we tense with quick gusts the way
        nesting birds are startled when branches rock
and tremble in rainstorms—and there comes a flickering
        light as the kitchen alternates dim and bright
with electric failure. Beside the dishwasher, a gold

glowing spot, the struggling emergency light, beats
        a surging kind of rhythm with Morse-code
ciphers, in dot-and-dash message, tied together
        in a chain linking dim thoughts of warm ease,
contrasted sharply with the storming blizzard blocked

from the orange fire by thin panes become translucent.
        By lamplight we read our books and hope
that our stereo is not forever damaged by power failure,
        as we wait for the calm end of blowing snowflakes.
Next morning, we shovel paths that lead us to the world.

Acknowledgments

There are many individuals besides myself who contributed significantly to making the publication of this book possible. I thank all who helped in any way.

There are a few people, however, whom I would like to especially thank for their unwavering support.

Vince Gotera has always been steadfast and an incomparable advisor, mentor, teacher, and friend. His constant encouragement and editorial judgement made all the difference.

Barbara Lounsberry has always given me exceptional support as a mentor, teacher and friend, as well. She has willingly done many favors to help my writing career along.

Grant Tracey and Phyllis Carlin both spent much time and effort reading and critiquing the first several drafts.

My son, Ron Sandvik, was always available to help me with my many computer difficulties—much of it operator error—and to help me decide which path to try next in my writing journey.

Steve Semken has been a creative and knowledgeable editor/publisher, willing to explain much about a first-time book.

My classmates and classes at the University of Northern Iowa, the Hearst Center for the Arts and the Waterloo Center for the Arts made insightful suggestions that improved my poetry.

I thank my children and their significant others for their encouragement and generous support: Ron and Georgia Sandvik, and their children, Kyri, Carson and Colton; Loren Sandvik and Lisa Darty; Katrina Sandvik and Jay Ratcliff.

I am especially grateful to Leonard—my best friend and the love of my life.

I gratefully acknowledge the editors of the *North American Review* where the poem "Sweet Fruits" first appeared.

I thank the judges and editors of *Lyrical Iowa* where the poems "Cat Eyes", "Seasons" and "Red-Winged Blackbird Migration I" first appeared in slightly altered forms.

Photo taken by Katrina Sandvik

Myrna Sandvik grew up on a traditional family farm near Lake City, Iowa, where her parents still live. She taught English and speech and French in high schools in the Cedar Falls area and later taught at Hawkeye Community College and the University of Northern Iowa. She was an editorial assistant for the *North American Review* for three years. At present, she is teaching adult creative writing at the Hearst Center for the Arts in Cedar Falls.

Sandvik has earned the BA, MAE and MA degrees, all from the University of Northern Iowa. She has had several poems printed in *Lyrical Iowa,* which is published by the Iowa Poetry Association and one poem published in the *North American Review,* a literary journal.

Sandvik has three grown children, Ron, Loren, and Katrina. She also has three grandchildren Kyri, Carson, and Colton. She lives with her husband, Leonard, on a small acreage near Brandon, Iowa, where she writes and gardens.

The Ice Cube Press began publishing in 1993 to focus on how to best live with the natural world as well as searching for stories about things being lost, or forgotten in Iowa. Since establishing the press we've been recognized by a number of well known writers including Gary Snyder, Gene Logsdon, Wes Jackson, Annie Dillard & Barry Lopez. We've published a fair number of well known authors as well, including, Mary Swander, Jim Heynen, Stephanie Mills, Bill McKibben & Paul Gruchow. Check out our books on our web site, at bookstores, or museum shops and see why we are dedicated to "hearing the other side." As always, I give thanks to Fenna and Laura!

Ice Cube Press 205 N Front Street
North Liberty, Iowa 52317-9302
p 319/626-2055 f 413/451-0223 c 319/558-7609
steve@icecubepress.com
www.icecubepress.com